Regions of the United States: The Pacific States

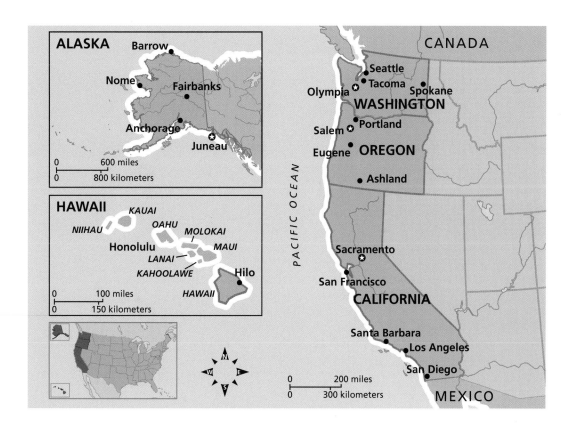

Stephen Feinstein

Raintree
Chicago, Illinois

© 2006 Raintree
Published by Raintree, a division of Reed Elsevier, Inc.
Chicago, Illinois

Customer Service 888-363-4266

Visit our website at www.heinemannraintree.com

Produced for Raintree by
White-Thomson Publishing Ltd,
Bridgewater Business Centre,
210 High Street, Lewes, BN7 2NH

For information, address the publisher:
Raintree, 100 N. LaSalle, Suite 1200, Chicago, IL 60602

Page layout by Clare Nicholas
Photo research by Stephen White-Thomson
Illustrations by John Fleck

11 10 09 08 07
10 9 8 7 6 5 4 3 2 1

**Library of Congress
Cataloging-in-Publication Data**

Feinstein, Stephen.
  The Pacific states / Stephen Feinstein.
      p. cm. -- (Regions of the USA)
  Includes bibliographical references and index.
  ISBN 1-4109-2310-X (hc) -- ISBN 1-4109-2318-5 (pb)
  1. Pacific States--Juvenile literature. 2. Alaska--Juvenile literature.
  3. Hawaii--Juvenile literature. I. Title. II. Series.
  F851.F44 2007
  979--dc22
                            2006004813

Acknowledgments
The publisher would like to thank the following for permission to reproduce photographs:
pp. 4, 5, 13, 21A, 23, 24B, 44 Ron Niebrugge; pp. 6, 15A, 15B, 22, 36A Topfoto; pp. 8, 12, 17B, 18A, 18–19, 24A, 28–29,
29A, 30, 31, 34, 35, 46, 47, 49, 50–51 Kerrick James; pp. 9, 17A, 33, 40, 43, 48, 50A, 51A Gibson Stock Photography; pp.
10, 26, 38, 39, 41A David Frazier; p. 11 David Muench/Corbis; pp. 14, 25, 27A, 41B Jeff Greenberg; p. 20 Dan Fletcher/I-
stock; p. 21B Marco Kopp/I-stock; p. 27B San Diego Scenics; p. 32 Natalie Fobes/Corbis; pp. 36–37, 42B Viesti Assocs; p.
42A Gabrielle Chan/I-stock; p. 45 Paul Topp/I-stock

Cover photo of Golden Gate Bridge, San Francisco reproduced with permission of Kerrick James

Contents

Some words are shown in bold, **like this.** You can find out what they mean by looking in the glossary.

The Pacific

Where is the highest mountain in North America? Where is the lowest point in the United States? Where are the tallest trees on earth? These amazing features can be found in the westernmost part of the United States, in the states that make up the Pacific region.

The Pacific region stretches from California north to Oregon and Washington, then way up north to Alaska, and then across the Pacific Ocean to Hawaii. Each year millions of visitors are drawn to this region's magnificent waterfalls, active volcanoes, burning deserts, lush tropical jungles and rainforests, huge **glaciers**, and spectacular coasts.

State names

The states in the Pacific region have different sources for their names. Alaska comes from *Alyeska*, a word meaning "great land" used by the **Aleut** people. California comes from a book from 1510 called *The Adventures of Esplandian* that featured a place called California. Hawaii is named after Hawaii Loa, a navigator who discovered the islands in the 400s. Oregon may come from French word *ouragan*, meaning "storm" or "hurricane." Washington is named for President George Washington.

The Athabascan Indians called Mount McKinley "Denali," the "High One" or "Great One." At 20,320 feet (6,194 meters), Mount McKinley in Alaska's Denali National Park is the highest mountain in North America.

▼

Pacific Coast Highway

To get a feel for the region, imagine driving up Route 1, California's Pacific Coast Highway. In some places, Route 1 hugs the sides of mountains. Each bend in the twisting road reveals breathtaking views of cliffs and steep, forested slopes falling away to the sea far below. At other spots along the way, Route 1 comes to within a few feet of the water's edge. It is possible to park the car and sunbathe on a sandy beach, where the only sounds are the cries of seagulls rising above the crashing surf.

Route 1 goes along every turn of the California coast, from San Diego in the south, to rugged forests in the north.
▼

Find out later...

What are these people waiting in line to see?

From which country do these traditional costumes come?

What are these people celebrating?

5

The eruption of Washington's Mount St. Helens on May 18, 1980, blasted away the top of the mountain and transformed it into a gray smoking crater.

Volcanoes and earthquakes

On May 18, 1980, Mount St. Helens in Washington exploded with a mighty roar. The deadly eruption caused hundreds of millions of dollars in damage, buried towns in eastern Washington under seven inches (18 centimeters) of volcanic ash, and took the lives of 57 people.

Like Washington, the other states of the Pacific region—California, Oregon, Alaska, and Hawaii—rest on shaky ground. Each state has a history of volcanic eruptions and earthquakes. The Hawaiian Islands were actually formed millions of years ago by volcanic eruptions. Visitors to Hawaii Volcanoes National Park on the island of Hawaii can view lava flowing from Kilauea, the world's most active volcano. Conditions surrounding volcanoes are constantly changing, so a safe viewing area for tourists today can be dangerous tomorrow or the next day.

California quakes

On April 18, 1906, a huge earthquake measuring 8.3 on the Richter scale hit San Francisco. The **Richter scale**, named after Dr. Charles F. Richter, is used to express the energy released by an earthquake. A measurement of 7 signals a major earthquake, and an 8 (10 times stronger than a 7) causes great destruction.

Most of the buildings that were still standing after the 60 seconds of the quake were then destroyed in the great fire that followed. An even greater earthquake, measuring 9.2—the most powerful earthquake ever recorded in North America—destroyed much of Anchorage, Alaska, on March 27, 1964.

Tsunamis

The Alaska earthquake of 1964 caused a **tsunami** that wiped out nearly every coastal village in south-central Alaska. In Hawaii a tsunami destroyed much of the city of Hilo in 1946 and again in 1960.

ALASKA

Barrow
Nome
Fairbanks
Anchorage
Juneau

0 — 600 miles
0 — 800 kilometers

HAWAII

KAUAI
NIIHAU
OAHU
MOLOKAI
Honolulu
LANAI   MAUI
KAHOOLAWE
HAWAII   Hilo

0 — 100 miles
0 — 150 kilometers

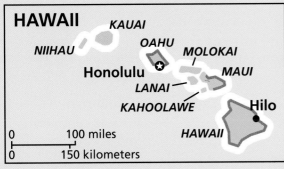

N
W   E
S

CANADA

Seattle
Olympia   Tacoma
Spokane
WASHINGTON

Salem   Portland
Eugene   OREGON

Ashland

PACIFIC OCEAN

Sacramento
San Francisco
CALIFORNIA

Santa Barbara
Los Angeles
San Diego

MEXICO

0 — 200 miles
0 — 300 kilometers

Fact file

State	Population	Size
Alaska	626,932	591,004 sq. mi. (1,530,700 sq. km)
California	33,871,648	158,648 sq. mi. (410,896 sq. km)
Hawaii	1,211,537	6,459 sq. mi. (16,729 sq. km)
Oregon	3,421,399	97,131 sq. mi. (251,569 sq. km)
Washington	5,894,121	70,637 sq. mi. (182,950 sq. km)

Tectonic plates

The earth's crust is made up of giant **tectonic plates** that are slowly moving. Beneath the western edge of the United States, two great slabs of the earth's crust called tectonic plates slowly grind against each other. The rubbing together of the plates causes earthquakes.

People and History

San Francisco's Chinatown

Visitors walking the crowded, narrow streets and alleys of San Francisco's Chinatown may feel as if they are in China. Many Chinese restaurants can be found here as well as Chinese food markets, herbalist shops, garment factories, galleries featuring jade carvings and other art from China, and souvenir shops.

The variety of the Pacific region's natural wonders is matched only by the ethnic diversity of the region's population. People from all over the world are drawn by the region's beauty and its many recreational and employment opportunities. California is the nation's most **populous** state. Within California, Los Angeles has large communities of people of Mexican, African-American, Korean, Chinese, and Japanese **descent**. San Francisco has a **diverse** ethnic mix, including large numbers of Hispanic, Chinese, and other Asian people. Other cities in the Pacific region are equally diverse.

San Francisco's Chinatown is the largest community of Chinese people anywhere outside of China.
▼

Fact file
A total of 12 percent of Americans live in California.

Asian influence

The Pacific region's **culture** and food have been strongly influenced by Asians. Alaska's first inhabitants came from Asia. Their descendents, Alaska's native peoples, make up about 16 percent of the state's population. Asians make up more than 11 percent of the state population of California. In Hawaii more than 40 percent of the population is descended from Asian people such as Chinese, Filipino, Japanese, Korean, and Vietnamese.

Hawaiian diversity

Hawaii is the most racially mixed state in the country. Japanese Americans make up about 20 percent of the population. Native Hawaiians of Polynesian descent make up another 20 percent of the population. Polynesian people come from Polynesia, a grouping of more than 1,000 islands scattered around the Pacific Ocean.

Hawaiians take pride in their cultural **traditions**. Native Hawaiians of Polynesian descent take part in a canoe pageant at the Polynesian Cultural Center on the island of Oahu, Hawaii.

Bone from the distant past

Scientists believe the first Alaskans were Athabascans. Scientists discovered an ancient tool probably belonging to the Athabascans. It was a caribou bone with a sharp edge. The scientists found it at a place called Old Crow in the Yukon, just east of Alaska. They believe the bone is 27,000 years old!

Early migration

Scientists believe the history of people in the Pacific region stretches back 40,000 years to the last **Ice Age**. Sea levels were much lower then. A **land bridge** connected Asia to Alaska. The first people to cross the land bridge from Asia into North America were **nomadic hunters** following herds of wild animals. While some of the hunters remained in Alaska, others went south. By about 12,000 years ago, the first hunters entered what are now the states of Washington, Oregon, and California. Hundreds of different groups settled in this region.

Nomadic people hunted mammoths, which are today extinct. These mammoth models were created from mammoth bones found in the La Brea Tar Pits in Los Angeles.

Ancient sailors

Between 4,000 and 10,000 years ago, the Inuit (also known as Eskimos) and Aleut came to Alaska. The land bridge no longer existed, so they crossed from Asia to Alaska by boat. Descendants of the Inuit and Aleut continue to live in Alaska.

Much later, about 1,500 years ago, Polynesians from the Marquesas Islands in the middle of the Pacific Ocean sailed 2,000 miles to the Hawaiian Islands in huge canoes. The first Hawaiians were then joined about 1,000 years ago by Polynesians from Tahiti.

Ancient pictographs in southern California were painted on the rock walls of caves and canyons.

▼

Petroglyphs and pictographs

Scientists believe that California Indians began using the bow and arrow around 300 A.D., because that is when the bow and arrow first appeared in their **petroglyphs** (carvings on rock). The oldest petroglyphs in Southern California are about 3,000 years old, and the earliest **pictographs** (paintings on rock) are about 1,500 years old.

Explorers, missionaries, and traders

The native peoples of Alaska, Washington, Oregon, and California thrived for thousands of years. Then the Europeans arrived, eventually taking away much of the native people's land and forcing them to change the way they lived.

Spaniards in California

In the 1700s Spanish priests established a chain of 21 **missions** extending from San Diego north to Sonoma, California. The missionaries enslaved Native Americans, forcing them into hard labor. The mission system ended in 1834. In 1848 the United States won a three-year war with Mexico. It gained a vast territory that included California and all the lands stretching eastward to Texas. California became a state two years later, in 1850.

The oldest building in San Francisco

The Mission San Francisco de Asis (now called Mission Dolores), the sixth mission founded by Father Junipero Serra, was built in 1769 in what is now the heart of San Francisco's Mission District. At the time, however, the city of San Francisco did not yet exist. The mission was rebuilt in 1782.

Mission Santa Barbara is a beautiful building. It was established by Spanish missionaries on December 4, 1786.

Russians in Alaska

Meanwhile, Russians established settlements in Alaska. In 1741 Vitus Bering, leading an expedition on behalf of Russia's ruler Peter the Great, reached the coast of Alaska. Russian fur traders and hunters arrived next, making slaves of the native Aleuts.

Americans reach the Pacific

In 1805 the Lewis and Clark expedition reached the Pacific Coast. A few years later, American fur traders began arriving in the lands that are now Washington and Oregon. At the time, England and the United States both claimed the area. In 1846 the two countries reached a final agreement on the official northern border of the United States. Oregon became a state in 1859 and Washington in 1889.

When Lewis and Clark reached the Pacific Coast, they built Fort Clatsop. This is one of the rooms inside a modern reconstruction of the original log building.

In the 1900s California's beautiful scenery, mild **climate**, and available jobs drew waves of **immigration** from east, west, and south. Washington, Oregon, Hawaii, and eventually Alaska would also attract immigrants. Alaska became a state in 1959.

Today, people still pan for gold in the streams of California and Alaska. These people are hoping to find gold in a stream near Fairbanks, Alaska.

Settlers and seekers of gold

From the 1840s to the 1860s, more than 300,000 settlers traveled west along the Oregon Trail, which ran 2,000 miles from Independence, Missouri, to Oregon City. Thousands of people also flocked to California, many from as far away as China. They were hoping to strike it rich after gold was discovered at Sutter's Mill in January 1848.

Gold seekers moved into lands of the Native Americans, often killing those who got in their way and enslaving others. Conflict between Native Americans and white settlers continued in the area. Another gold rush, this time in Alaska, began when gold was discovered near Dawson City in the Klondike region of the Yukon in 1897.

Change comes to Hawaii

In 1778 Captain James Cook accidentally landed in Hawaii. He was the first European to land there. This would cost him his life, because he was killed in a dispute with the Hawaiians. Within a few years of Cook's arrival, trading ships and whalers were stopping in Hawaii to take on supplies. Hawaii's isolation ended shortly after that, with the arrival of missionaries and white settlers. Sugar plantations imported workers from Japan, China, and other places. The islands that make up Hawaii became a U.S. territory in 1898, and gained statehood in 1959.

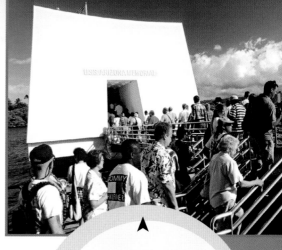

Visitors take a tour of the U.S.S. Arizona National Memorial, which floats atop the remains of a battleship that sank during Japan's attack on Pearl Harbor.

James Cook was an Englishman who was seeking a **northwest passage** between the Atlantic and Pacific Oceans when he came ashore in Hawaii.

The Pacific region in World War II

On December 7, 1941, the Japanese bombed Pearl Harbor in Honolulu, which led to the entry of the United States into World War II. The next year, Japan attacked Alaska's Aleutian Islands, invading Attu and Kiska. The Japanese were defeated there by U.S. troops the following year.

Land in the Area

Alaska, the great land

Alaska is 591,004 square miles (1,530,700 square kilometers) of mainly wilderness. Alaska has scenery on a grand scale—17 of the 20 highest mountains in the United States, 39 mountain ranges, 80 volcanoes, more than three million lakes, 3,000 rivers, and 100,000 glaciers. Alaska's 33,904-mile (54,563-kilometer) coastline is longer than the rest of the country's coastlines combined.

The writer Mark Twain described the Hawaiian Islands as "the loveliest fleet of islands that lies anchored to any ocean." Hawaii, more than 2,000 miles west of California, is a chain of 132 islands. The eight most important islands are Hawaii, Maui, Kahoolawe, Lanai, Molokai, Oahu, Kauai, and Niihau. The islands have tropical vegetation, mountains and cliffs, waterfalls, volcanoes, and palm-fringed beaches.

Washington's Puget Sound also contains many islands, including the 172 forest-covered San Juan Islands. Alaska, too, has islands—more than 1,800—including the Aleutian Islands, Kodiak Island, and the forested islands in the Panhandle of Southeast Alaska.

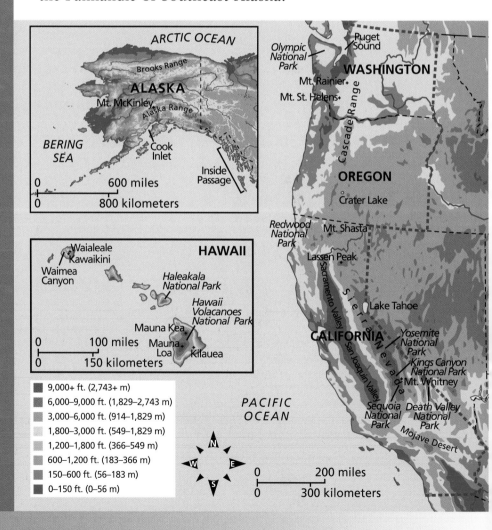

Unusual lakes

In the southern part of the Cascade Mountains in Oregon is a lake so perfectly round and of such a deep blue color that it seems unreal. Crater Lake, the deepest lake in the United States, was formed more than 7,000 years ago, when the top of a volcano exploded. The resulting crater filled with water from surrounding glaciers.

Lake Tahoe in the Sierra Nevada mountain range in eastern California is North America's largest mountain lake. Mono Lake, just east of the Sierra Nevada, is in the middle of a huge **salt flat**.

Spectacular Waimea Canyon on the island of Kauai, Hawaii, from an aerial view.

The "Grand Canyon of the Pacific"

Waimea Canyon on the island of Kauai, Hawaii, is often referred to as the "Grand Canyon of the Pacific." The river-cut gorge is ten miles long, a mile wide, and more than a half mile deep. The Waimea River winds its way along the bottom of the canyon. The brilliant color of the canyon walls comes from the deep-red earth.

Oregon's breathtakingly beautiful Crater Lake is often covered with snow in winter.

Volcanoes

Volcanoes pepper almost the entire Pacific region. Alaska has 80 volcanoes. The Cascade Range consists of a chain of mighty volcanoes reaching from northern Washington down through Oregon and into northern California. The Hawaiian Islands themselves were formed by lava bubbling up from the ocean. Two volcanoes on the island of Hawaii are still active—Mauna Loa and Kilauea. At 13,677 feet (4,100 meters), the top of Mauna Loa is cold enough to be covered by snow in the winter. Visitors can get close enough to see the flows of lava that often pour out of the volcanoes.

An eruption of Kilauea in the Hawaii Volcanoes National Park, on Hawaii's Big Island.

The Cascade volcanoes

The best-known volcanoes in the Cascade mountain range include Washington's Mount Adams, Mount Baker, Mount Rainier, and Mount St. Helens, Oregon's Mount Hood, and California's Mount Shasta and Mount Lassen.

Mountains to Deserts

Yosemite National Park in the Sierra Nevada, a range of mountains in eastern California, is one of the country's most popular tourist destinations. In Yosemite Valley spectacular waterfalls thunder down to the valley floor from atop towering granite walls.

California's Death Valley National Park is larger than the state of Connecticut. In it is the lowest point in North America, at Badwater, which is 282 feet (86 meters) below sea level. Just 80 miles (129 kilometers) away is Mount Whitney, the highest point in California, at 14,497 feet (4,419 meters).

Some like it hot!

Death Valley is so hot in the summer that people used to go there only in the winter. But now Death Valley has begun to attract brave vacationers who like a challenge. Perhaps they enjoy such activities as boiling eggs on the ground. However, people who do not enjoy walking around in 120 to 130 °F (49 to 55 °C) temperatures should avoid Death Valley in the summer.

Around the edges of California's Mono Lake are strange rock formations called tufa. The tufa formed underwater when salty lake water combined with fresh spring water bubbling up from below. The lake level eventually dropped, revealing the weird formations.

Weather and climate

From arctic Alaska to the burning deserts of southern California to the tropical rainforests of Hawaii, the Pacific region includes all possible types of climates and weather conditions.

California has a rainy season and a dry season. Throughout most of California, it hardly ever rains in the summer but winters can be very rainy. In summer the Pacific Ocean acts as a natural air conditioner along California's coast. Fog often rolls in from the Pacific, keeping temperatures cool. But just a few miles inland, the weather is hot and dry under a blazing sun.

Summer in San Francisco

In the summer San Francisco is the coldest city in the lower 48 states. Temperatures rarely climb above 70 °F (21 °C). Tourists waiting to ride the **cable cars** can be seen shivering in their summer clothes.

Hawaii's warm weather and beautiful beaches draw vacationers from all over the world.

Midnight sun

In summer in Alaska, the farther north you go, the longer the days are. Barrow, America's northernmost city, sits on the coast of the Arctic Ocean. There, the sun does not set from May 10 to August 2. During the winter the opposite occurs. Instead of the Midnight Sun, from November 18 to January 23 there is darkness at noon and bitter cold. In 1971 it was −80 °F (-60 °C) in Prospect Creek, the coldest temperature ever recorded in Alaska. On such a day a person's breath turns to ice crystals.

Fact file
Nearly 500 inches (1,270 centimeters) of rain fall each year on Waialeale and Kawaikini, high peaks in the center of the island of Kauai, Hawaii.

▲ The aurora borealis, or northern lights, is a familiar sight in the night skies of Alaska during winter. It can sometimes also be seen in the lower 48 states.

Northern Lights

The aurora borealis, or northern lights, appear as shimmering bands and curtains of color in the night sky. The aurora occurs when electrically charged particles from the sun cause a glow in the upper layer of the earth's atmosphere.

▲ Alaska's mountains are covered in snow.

Animals and Plants

Because of its extreme temperatures and habitats, the Pacific Region is home to a diverse population of animals and plants.

Bear country

At one time, grizzly bears roamed California. The grizzly is such an important part of the state's heritage it is the official state animal. But don't expect to find a grizzly in California. The last one died in 1922. The grizzly bear disappeared in California after the gold rush, when miners, ranchers, and settlers began to shoot them. California still has a large population of black bears. To see grizzly bears in the wild, head for Alaska.

The condor makes a comeback

The California condor, North America's largest bird with a 9-foot (2.75-meter) wingspan, was in danger of becoming extinct. Beginning in 1980 scientists caught each of the remaining 27 condors and started a breeding program. In 1992 they began releasing condors raised in captivity. By 2005 more than 185 condors had been released into the wild.

Grizzly bears hunt salmon in Alaskan rivers. Grizzly bears can be found from southeast Alaska to the Arctic Circle.

Whale watching

Whale watching, from shore or on a boat, is a popular activity on and off the coasts of all states in the Pacific region. In Alaska's waters alone, twenty different kinds of whales can be found. Off the coast of California, gray whales, humpback whales, and blue whales are a common sight. Boats can get very close to a whale. A thrilling moment known as **breaching** occurs when a whale leaps out of the water and crashes back down.

▶ This humpback whale is breaching. Whales migrate along the Pacific Coast from California all the way up to Alaska. Whale watchers can also spot the enormous animals in Hawaiian waters.

Living near mountain lions

Because mountain lions in California cannot be hunted for sport, their population has increased. Since humans live in areas that used to be wild, sightings of mountain lions are becoming more frequent. On certain hiking trails, signs advise how to behave when encountering a mountain lion.

Unique trees

The Pacific region has many types of plants that can be found nowhere else on Earth. California's redwoods are the tallest trees in the world and **giant sequoias** in the Sierra Nevada are the biggest. The giant sequoias are between 1,800 and 2,700 years old. These trees are young compared to California's **bristlecone pines**. Found in the White Mountains, many of these bent and twisted trees are more than 4,000 years old!

One strange-looking tree is the Joshua tree in California's Mojave Desert. It grows at odd angles and its twisted branches look like outstretched human arms. The Joshua tree soaks up water during rare rainfalls and stores it for months.

Giant sequoias grow in California's Sierra Nevada mountain range.

The Joshua tree can live for 200 years or more.

The world's tallest trees

The redwood trees of Northern California are the tallest trees in the world. One of them in the Tall Trees Grove of Redwood National Park is 368 feet (112 meters) tall, about as high as a 30-story building.

Tropical trees and flowers

Hawaii's state tree, the kukui, is also called the candlenut tree. Oil from the kukui is used to make candles and dyes. Hawaii also has many colorful flowers, including hundreds of different kinds of orchids.

Tiny trees of the tundra

While Sitka spruce in southeast Alaska grow more than 200 feet (61 meters) high, severe cold and wind stunt the growth of trees on the tundra. It is common to find full-grown trees that are only 18 inches high (46 centimeters) and 0.5 inches (1.27 centimeters) across.

Flowers, especially orchids, are part of the traditional dress of native Hawaiians.

The Olympic Rain Forest

The Olympic Rain Forest in Washington's Olympic National Park is almost always wet and cool. The trees in this forest are mainly Sitka spruce and western hemlock. They are mostly covered with moss. Rainfall in the park ranges from 12 to 14 feet (3.75 to 4.25 meters) every year.

Cities and Towns

Several large cities, from San Diego, California, to Seattle, Washington, lie along the western coast of the United States. These and the many smaller cities and towns in between are places people like to visit as they drive along the Pacific Coast.

San Diego

San Diego is just north of the Mexican border. At the famous San Diego Zoo in Balboa Park, giant pandas Shi Shi and Bai Yun draw admiring crowds. Old Town San Diego and the Gaslamp Quarter give a feel of the city's Spanish influences and early history. Many **Victorian** homes in the Gaslamp Quarter are surrounded by real gas lamps and brick sidewalks. San Diego has miles of beautiful sandy beaches.

Take the trolley to Mexico

San Diego's Blue Line Trolley (unofficially called the Tijuana Trolley) runs south through downtown San Diego to within 100 feet (30 meters) of the Mexican border. A bus then takes passengers to downtown Tijuana, Mexico, just 17 miles (27 kilometers) from San Diego. There they can dine and shop in this bustling Mexican border town.

The view from San Diego's harbor shows the city's dramatic skyline.
▼

Los Angeles

About 150 miles (241 kilometers) north of San Diego, Los Angeles, the nation's second largest city, extends across a huge space between the mountains and the ocean. To many people Los Angeles is a city of endless beaches in the sun, surfers waiting for the perfect wave, laid-back living, and Hollywood movie stars. Los Angeles is known for its cultural diversity. People have come to Los Angeles from all over the world, especially Mexico and many Asian countries, to make a better life.

Most of the streets in Palm Springs, California, are lined with palm trees.

Fact file:
More artists, actors, dancers, musicians, writers, and filmmakers live in Los Angeles than any other city in the world.

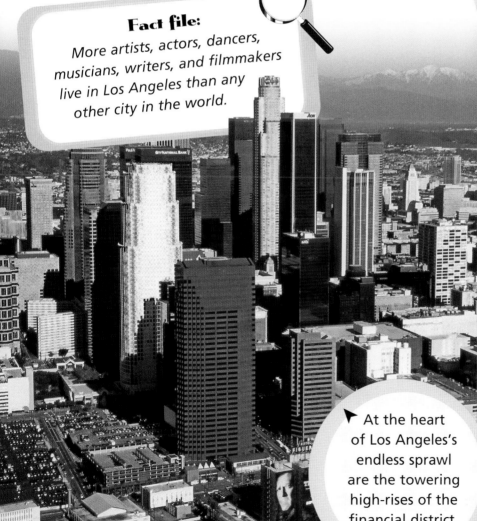

Palm Springs

The small desert town of Palm Springs has hundreds of golf courses. But it is not necessary to play golf to have a good time there. An aerial tramway leads up to the Mountain Station at 8,516 feet (2,596 meters) and offers stunning views.

▼ At the heart of Los Angeles's endless sprawl are the towering high-rises of the financial district.

Golden Gate Park

From the 1870s through the 1890s, John McLaren, a Scottish landscape gardener, transformed a wasteland of shifting sand dunes belonging to the city of San Francisco into Golden Gate Park. Visitors from all over the world admire the park's beautiful trees and plants and a dozen artificial lakes. There are also several museums, an aquarium, an **arboretum**, and a Japanese Tea Garden.

San Francisco

San Francisco sits at the northern end of a **peninsula**, surrounded by water on three sides. It is a city with impossibly steep hills and Victorian houses that are sometimes referred to as "painted ladies" because of their bright colors. Fog from the Pacific Ocean often drifts across the city, causing the tops of tall buildings and the Golden Gate Bridge to disappear from view. The air is often filled with typical San Francisco sounds—the crying of the seagulls, the clanging of cable cars as they slowly climb up the hills, and the distant booming of a foghorn.

San Francisco is famous for its "painted ladies," or Victorian homes. Many of the city's Victorian homes were destroyed during the 1906 earthquake, but thousands of them remain, including many that were rebuilt.

The Bay Area

The San Francisco Bay Area consists of many small and large cities that border San Francisco Bay. The largest include San Jose, San Francisco, Oakland, and Berkeley. The Berkeley campus of the University of California is one of the nation's leading educational centers. Artwork and exhibits at the Oakland Museum of California trace the state's natural and cultural history. San Jose is now known as the "Capital of Silicon Valley," because it is the home of so many high tech companies. The Bay Area, which covers nine California counties, also includes military bases, busy airports, and many parks.

Passengers cling to a cable car as it slowly climbs a steep San Francisco hill.

Muir Woods

Across the Golden Gate Bridge and to the northwest is Muir Woods National Monument. It is the closest redwood grove to San Francisco. Trails run along a creek and up the slopes of Mount Tamalpais. Visitors wander through the silent redwood grove stretching their necks to look up at the giant redwoods towering over them.

29

Sailing from Seattle

Visitors can take ferries from Seattle's waterfront to many of the islands in Puget Sound. Puget Sound is an arm of the Pacific Ocean that extends inland for about 90 miles (144 kilometers).

Portland, Oregon

Portland, Oregon, is known as the Rose City because its roses bloom year-round. On clear days the snowy peak of Mount Hood is visible to the east of Portland. The Pearl District is a neighborhood with art galleries, boutiques, and restaurants.

Seattle, Washington

Seattle is often called the Emerald City because its rainy climate keeps the city green year-round. A **monorail** leads from downtown Seattle to the 600-foot (183-meter) landmark Space Needle. The amazing views from the top include the Olympic Mountains to the west and mighty snow-covered Mount Rainier to the east.

Seattle's soaring Space Needle was built for the 1962 World's Fair to reflect the world's future in space.

Honolulu, Hawaii

In the Hawaiian language, *honolulu* means "sheltered bay" or "place of shelter." Honolulu is Hawaii's capital and largest city. It can be found on the island of Oahu. Big hotels line two-and-a-half miles (4 kilometers) of Waikiki Beach in Honolulu. Millions of visitors a year are attracted to Waikiki's hotels, shops, and nightlife. Just west of Waikiki is Ala Moana Center, the world's largest open-air shopping center. The Honolulu Academy of Arts near downtown Honolulu features the largest collection of Western and Asian art in Hawaii.

At sunrise only a few people wander along Waikiki Beach in Honolulu, Hawaii. Later in the day, thousands of people will crowd the beach to enjoy the sun and surf. ▼

Juneau, Alaska

The small town of Juneau, Alaska, is the nation's only state capital that has no roads leading in or out. The only way to get to Juneau is by boat or plane.

Rural Life

Scattered across Alaska's vast wilderness are people who live a rural life in remote cabins. Many of them are hundreds of miles from the nearest road. Their only contact with the outside world is through pilots who deliver mail and supplies on small planes.

Giant vegetables

Farm families in the Matanuska Valley north of Anchorage benefit from the many hours of extra sunlight during Alaska's short growing season. They have grown huge vegetables, such as 90-pound (41-kilogram) cabbages and 30-pound (13.6-kilogram) turnips!

The Inuit

Rural Alaskans include the Inuit people, who live in remote villages by the Bering Sea and Arctic Ocean. The traditional Inuit diet consisted of marine mammals, caribou, birds, and fish. Inuit homes, built partly underground, were made of driftwood, antlers, whalebones, and sod. The Inuit also built snow-block igloos as temporary shelters in the winter, when they traveled by dogsled. Today's Inuit enjoy many aspects of modern life, such as television and snowmobiles.

Alaska's fishing industry employs many native Alaskan fishers.

Home on the range

Large ranches have long been part of rural life in eastern Washington and Oregon, as well as parts of California. Large farms in California's San Joaquin, Sacramento, and Imperial Valleys rely on **migrant** workers to harvest crops.

One of America's biggest cattle ranches is actually on Hawaii's Big Island, a place better known for its volcanoes and beautiful beaches. The Parker Ranch was started in 1847 by John Parker. Today, modern cowboys in Hawaii live a rural lifestyle that harks back to the days of the Old West. The Hawaiian cowboys ride the range on horseback, herding 50,000 head of cattle on the Parker Ranch's 350 square miles (906.5 square kilometers) of rolling grasslands.

Modern cowboys at the historic Parker Ranch on Hawaii's Big Island catch cattle just like the cowboys of the ► old wild west.

Getting Around

San Francisco-Oakland Bay Bridge

The San Francisco-Oakland Bay Bridge was completed in 1936 in California. It connects San Francisco to Oakland. The double-decker bridge is 5.2 miles (8.4 kilometers) long. An upper and a lower deck were required because of the heavy traffic. During the 1989 Loma Prieta Earthquake, part of the bridge collapsed. It was repaired, but a new, safer span for the eastern part of the Bay Bridge is now being built to replace the old one.

Los Angeles has 27 freeways, more than any other city in America. The city's first freeway, the Pasadena Freeway, was built in 1945. It was called a "stopless motorway" and was designed to speed cars along at 45 miles (72.5 kilometers) per hour.

The Golden Gate

The Golden Gate Bridge opened for traffic in 1937. From it, fantastic views of the city, the bay, and the ocean can be seen. In 1937 the Golden Gate Bridge was the world's longest suspension bridge, with a length of 1.7 miles (2.75 kilometers). Today, many suspension bridges are longer, but few can offer such wonderful views.

The beautiful Golden Gate Bridge connects San Francisco with Marin County to the north. More than 100,000 vehicles a day cross the bridge.

Ferries and airplanes

Many places in the Pacific region cannot be reached by road. For example, people must take a ferry to get to the San Juan Islands in Puget Sound, Washington. Many coastal towns and islands in Alaska's panhandle have a ferry service known as Alaska's Marine Highway.

To get to remote villages in the Alaskan wilderness, it is necessary to fly. The pilots are called bush pilots and they fly people, goods, and mail all around Alaska. Bush pilots even save people's lives in medical emergencies.

Travel by Dogsled

In the winter in Alaska, the best way to get around is by dogsled. A dogsled can move better than other types of transportation through the snowy wilderness. Traveling by dogsled is known as "mushing."

◄ An Alaskan bush pilot has landed his plane on a small lake near Mount McKinley.

Work in the Area

The Pacific region offers both traditional and modern jobs, ranging from high-tech jobs in natural resources to jobs in entertainment and television. Silicon Valley, the birthplace of the microchip (made from silicon) and the personal computer, is the name people have given to California's Santa Clara Valley. The area's high tech companies provide jobs for hundreds of thousands of people who develop computers, chips, websites, and software. Centers of high tech exist in other parts of the Pacific region, too, such as Seattle, Washington.

Steve Jobs, head of Apple Computer Company, launched the iPod mini at a computer event in San Francisco.

Change in the valley

Fifty years ago the area now known as Silicon Valley was filled with orchards and farms. Today, visitors would have a hard time finding any peach orchards as they drive by one high tech company after another, many of them housed in modern glass buildings.

The business

Los Angeles is the center of America's movie industry. The major Hollywood studios are located there, as are major television production studios. People in Los Angeles refer to the entertainment industry as "the business." Hollywood film and TV actors are not the only people who work in the business here. There are also scriptwriters, film editors, producers and directors, cinematographers, set designers, costume designers, make-up people, and many different types of technicians who work with sound, lighting, and props. Not everyone in Los Angeles works in the business, but many people do—at least 200,000.

The birth of Hollywood

The movie industry started in Hollywood in 1911 when New York film producer David Horsley shot *The Law of the Range,* a silent film, in Hollywood. Other film producers soon followed Horsley to Hollywood. They were attracted to southern California's warm, sunny climate and beautiful scenery, which were perfect for outdoor filming.

The Tech Museum in San Jose, California, is a great place to learn about Silicon Valley's high tech industry.

The benefits of oil in Alaska

State income from oil and gas pays for most of Alaska's government programs. Alaska has no income or sales tax. In 1982 the state government began making an annual payment—as much as $2,000 each year—to each of Alaska's residents. Alaska is the only state that pays this kind of return.

Natural resources

Many Pacific region workers find jobs in natural resource industries such as mining, lumber, fishing, and farming. About 10 billion apples are grown in Washington each year, more than in any other state. Although salmon in Washington waters declined dramatically due to overfishing, salmon are now being produced in commercial fish hatcheries there.

Alaska turned out to be very rich in natural resources and Seward's folly was the deal of the century. First came the gold rush. Then came the mining of copper, zinc, and coal. But the most valuable resource is Alaska's oil and natural gas, which provide 87 percent of the state's **revenue**. Alaska produces 500 million barrels of oil a year, about 23 percent of United States oil production.

Washington's greatest natural resource has always been its forests. Timber is sawed into logs in this Washington sawmill.

Feeding the nation

At least 25 percent of the nation's produce comes from farmland in California's Central Valley, which includes Sacramento Valley in the north and San Joaquin Valley in the south. The Pacific region is the center of the nation's strawberry production. California is world famous for its fine wines produced from grapes grown in the Napa and Sonoma Valleys, and in many other parts of the state. Washington is an important producer of apples. Hawaii is the nation's largest supplier of pineapples and an important producer of sugar.

Sun-dried tomatoes are just one of California's many agricultural products.

Taking in tourists

One important natural resource of the Pacific region is its natural beauty, which has given rise to a tourism boom. Millions of visitors travel to each one of the states in the Pacific region every year. California is one of the most visited states in the country. Hundreds of thousands of people living in California and throughout the region depend on tourism for their jobs.

Free Time

Experience Music Project

Frank Gehry, an architect famous for his unique and unusual designs for museums, designed Seattle's Experience Music Project to resemble a smashed guitar. The museum, which celebrates the past, present, and future of music, features a huge collection of artifacts belonging to rock legend Jimi Hendrix, who was from Seattle. There are also exhibits about the history of rock music and the development of the electric guitar.

Visitors will have no trouble finding their favorite kinds of music in the cities of the Pacific region. Jazz, pop/rock, blues, rap, and salsa are featured in clubs in big cities as well as smaller towns. Music festivals draw big crowds every year. Jazz fans head for the Monterey Jazz Festival in September. Since 1958 this annual festival in Monterey, California, has been a great place to enjoy all types of jazz music.

Keeping alive the spirit of California's Hispanic heritage, these girls in traditional Mexican dress are dancing at the Cinco de Mayo Celebration at historic Pueblo de Los Angeles, California.

Cities in the Pacific region also have world-class ballet companies and theaters, such as the Pacific Northwest Ballet in Seattle and Ashland, Oregon's open-air Elizabethan Theater.

This totem pole in Ketchikan, Alaska, is one of many similar examples of Native American wood carving that can be seen at Totem Bight State Historical Park. ➤

Visual arts

Pacific region art museums and galleries feature artists throughout the region as well as art from other times and places. Los Angeles' Getty Center is a spectacular complex of marble and stone. It sits high on a ridge above the city and the sea, and has one of the world's greatest collections of art. A tram carries visitors up to the Getty Center from the parking lot down below. In San Diego a unique Museum of Photographic Arts is located in Balboa Park.

Totem poles

Alaska's Tlingit and Haida Indians carved totem poles from huge cedar trees. There are more totem poles in Ketchikan than anywhere else in the world.

The huge Getty Center in Los Angeles took 13 years to build at a cost of $1 billion. It covers 110 acres (44.5 hectares) of land.

Food festivals

California's Garlic Festival in Gilroy is a popular annual event. Garlic lovers enjoy garlic milkshakes, garlic ice cream, and other garlic food items. Other annual Pacific region food festivals include the Pumpkin Festival in Half Moon Bay, California, and the Artichoke Festival in Castroville, California; Alaska's Kodiak Crab Festival; Hawaii's Kona Coffee Festival; and Oregon's Strawberry Festival in Lebanon, and the Seafood and Wine Festival in Newport.

Fans of dim sum say that San Francisco rivals Hong Kong in the popularity and quality of its dim sum restaurants.

Dim sum

Dim sum, served in Chinese restaurants, are pastry-like items filled with pork, shrimp, or vegetables that are steamed, fried, or baked. Some popular examples are baked pork buns, sesame rice dumplings, and steamed scallop dumplings.

This "garlic" person is one of the thousands of garlic lovers attending the annual Garlic Festival in Gilroy, California.

The influence of Mexico

California once belonged to Mexico, so it is not surprising that Mexican foods are very popular in California. Food items such as tacos, enchiladas, and burritos served with spicy salsa, can be found everywhere.

California cuisine

When Alice Waters opened her Chez Panisse restaurant in Berkeley, California, in 1971, people looking for a healthier way to eat had a new type of cooking to enjoy—California **cuisine**. Waters used the freshest and purest ingredients, many of them grown in her own garden. She combined ingredients to improve the natural flavors, for example preparing seared ahi tuna with sesame seeds and hot and sour raspberry sauce. Soon, California cuisine began appearing in restaurants throughout California, the Pacific region, and beyond.

These brightly colored vegetables are on display at the Farmer's Market in City Park in downtown Eugene, Oregon.

▼

Fusion foods

New combinations of different cooking styles are called "fusion" foods. For example, Pan-Asian cuisine features dishes that combine foods from several different Asian countries. One new type of cuisine created in California is called Cal-Asian. Cal-Asian foods are a fusion of Californian and Asian cooking that combines Asian and American foods into new kinds of dishes.

Dogsledding

Every winter in Alaska, adventurous dogsled drivers, known as "mushers," take part in the Iditarod Trail Sled Dog Race, a 1,100-mile (1,770-kilometer) race from Anchorage to Nome. Winning mushers include women such as Susan Butcher, who has won the race four times.

Winter sports

In the mountains of Alaska, Washington, Oregon, and California, heavy winter snows make for extremely long skiing seasons. It is even possible to ski in Hawaii. Mauna Kea, a volcano on the Big Island, is Hawaii's highest mountain, at 13,796 feet (4,205 meters). The volcano has not been active for more than 4,000 years. During the winter, the top part of Mauna Kea is covered with snow. It is often warm enough to go skiing there without wearing a jacket.

Extreme snowmobiling is one winter sport that experienced riders can enjoy in Chugach National Forest in Alaska.

Summer sports

Hiking and backpacking in the high country of the Sierra Nevada and the Cascade and Olympic Mountains is a favorite summer activity. The Pacific region's many lakes and seaside beaches are ideal for water sports—sailing, kayaking, swimming, windsurfing, and surfing. In Hawaii surfing is a year-round sport. Ancient stone petroglyphs picturing surfers have been found in Hawaii. In fact, surfing has been popular in Hawaii for hundreds of years.

This surfer is riding a tube wave in Hawaii.

San Francisco's new sports stadium

SBC Park (formerly Pacific Bell Park) on San Francisco's waterfront replaced Candlestick Park as the home of the San Francisco Giants in April 2000. The new stadium seats 42,000 spectators. Barry Bonds hit the first official Giants homerun on opening day, April 11, 2000. Bonds also hit his 500th, 600th, and 700th homeruns here.

Beverly Hills

Many movie stars live in a city next to Los Angeles called Beverly Hills. This is where tourists and locals alike are most likely to sneak a peek at the homes of Hollywood stars. In Beverly Hills the rich and famous shop on Rodeo Drive, which is known for its luxury stores. There are 900 stores in Beverly Hills, even though only about 33,000 people live there!

Star spotting

In the 1930s and 1940s, the intersection of Hollywood and Vine was the center of Hollywood night life. At that corner today is the Walk of Fame. More than 1,800 names of Hollywood celebrities are engraved in bronze stars set into the sidewalk. The names include Walt Disney, Ronald Reagan, and Tom Hanks. Meanwhile, Grauman's Chinese Theatre on Hollywood Boulevard has other reminders of Hollywood's stars. In the courtyard the footprints, handprints, and autographs of many Hollywood stars are pressed into the concrete floor.

Grauman's Chinese Theatre in Los Angeles, built in 1927, was designed to resemble a Chinese temple. ▶

The castle on the hill

Atop a hill above San Simeon along the central California coast is a famous castle that draws visitors from all over the world. In 1919 William Randolph Hearst, a wealthy newspaper publisher, hired the architect Julia Morgan to build his dream castle. The two worked on the project for the next 28 years. Hearst filled the castle with priceless artworks from all over Europe. The Hearst Castle consists of the 115-room Casa Grande and three other palaces, surrounded by gardens and fountains. Hearst invited many famous Hollywood film stars to spend their free time at his castle.

Hollywood Bowl

In July 1922, the Los Angeles Philharmonic Orchestra first played under the stars at the Hollywood Bowl. This natural arena can seat almost 18,000 guests. It has been the summer home for the Los Angeles Philharmonic since it first played there. During the Summer Festival season, music-lovers can purchase a ticket for just $1 for a seat at the top of the Bowl!

The magnificent Hearst Castle in San Simeon, California, was once the estate of newspaper publisher William Randolph Hearst.

Universal Studios

Covering 420 acres, Universal Studios in Hollywood is the largest movie studio in the world. A theme park was built around the studio. A tram tour shows visitors where and how movies are made, including demonstrations of special effects such as fires, explosions, avalanches, and earthquakes. More than 500 sets re-create many places around the world: New York City, European cities, Mexican villages, wild west towns, and ancient Egypt.

Theme parks

Disneyland, the original theme park, is located in Anaheim, California, just south of Los Angeles. Millions of people have been there since Walt Disney opened it for business in 1955.

Disney remains an important theme park in California, but there are many others dotted around the state. The state's climate and history as a tourist destination mean that it has many theme parks to offer. SeaWorld San Diego has marine life shows and rides. Six Flags Magic Mountain near Los Angeles has a selection of thrilling rides. Paramount's Great America and Six Flags Marine World, both near San Francisco, offer amazing coaster rides.

More than 33 million people enjoy rides such as this one in Disneyland in Anaheim, California, every year.

Festivals and holidays

Various annual festivals are held throughout the Pacific region. Seattle's Seafair, which lasts several weeks, offers boat races on Lake Washington, parades, and wandering clowns and pirates. There are also jazz concerts and other celebrations.

All peoples of the Pacific region celebrate special holidays. The Chinese New Year Parade in San Francisco is the largest celebration of its kind outside of Asia. Highlights include elaborately decorated floats, school marching bands, a martial arts group, stilt walkers, lion dancers, Chinese acrobatics, and the 200-foot-long (61-meter-long) Golden Dragon.

Old Spanish Days Fiesta, Santa Barbara

Every August the Old Spanish Days Fiesta takes place in Santa Barbara, California. The five-day event is a celebration of the city's Spanish heritage. There are parades, a carnival, a rodeo, herds of horses, musical performances, and two colorful marketplaces.

The Golden Dragon float that ends the traditional Chinese New Year's Parade in San Francisco is accompanied by more than 60,000 firecrackers.

An Amazing Region

The Pacific Crest Trail

Adventurous hikers with six months to spare can go all the way from the Mexican border to the Canadian border by following the Pacific Crest Trail. The trail runs through California, Oregon, and Washington. Hikers starting at the southern end of the trail must make their way through hot deserts. In the northern portions of the trail, they can either hike or ski through snowy mountains.

The Pacific region is a land of wild extremes including volcanic eruptions, earthquakes, tsunamis, North America's highest and lowest points and hottest and coldest temperatures, the world's wettest spot, and some of the world's driest regions. Within the vast region are burning deserts, frozen wilderness, countless islands, beautiful forests, spectacular mountain ranges, and tropical jungles.

Although thousands of miles of ocean separate Hawaii from the other four states, and Alaska is separated from Washington by Canadian territory, the five states of the Pacific region share a great deal.

Visitors climbing the giant sand dunes near Stovepipe Wells in California's Death Valley National Park could easily imagine they are hiking in the Sahara Desert of North Africa.

Many of the nation's finest colleges and universities are located in the states of the Pacific region. These are students on the campus of the University of California, Los Angeles.

A diverse people

All five states have ethnically diverse populations. California and Hawaii in particular have many people of Chinese, Japanese, and Korean descent. The culture and cuisine of the Pacific region is strongly influenced by Asia and Mexico.

The five states of the Pacific region have been a magnet for immigrants from all over the world. The movie industry of Los Angeles and the high technology industries based in Northern California's Silicon Valley and other places such as Seattle provide jobs for hundreds of thousands of people. The region's economies also include rich natural resources such as oil, minerals, and timber.

Ring of fire

The Pacific Rim is used to describe the countries that form a "rim" around the Pacific Ocean, including islands. In the United States, the states of the Pacific region are the only states that are part of the Pacific Rim. A "Ring of Fire" is said to extend all around the Pacific Rim. This is because there are active volcanoes all around the Pacific Rim.

These drummers are part of a West African dance performance in downtown Oakland, California.

Find Out More

World Wide Web

The Fifty States
www.infoplease.com/states.html
This website has a clickable U.S. map that gives facts about each of the 50 states, plus images of each state's flag.

These sites have pictures, statistics, and other facts about each state in the Pacific region:

Alaska.com
www.alaskaonline.com

Welcome to California
www.ca.gov

Hawaii.com
www.hawaii.com

Oregon Historical Society
www.ohs.org

Washington State History Museum
www.wshs.org

Books to read

Blashfield, Jean F. *Washington*. Danbury, Conn.: Children's Press, 2001.

Bredeson, Carmen. *Mount St. Helens Volcano: Violent Eruption*. Berkeley Heights, N.J.: Enslow Publishers, 2001.

Burgan, Michael. *California*. Estes Park, Colo.: Benchmark Investigative Group, 2002.

Ingram, Scott. *California: The Golden State*. Milwaukee: Gareth Stevens, 2002.

Johnston, Joyce. *Alaska*. Minneapolis: Lerner Publications, 2001.

Somervill, Barbara A. *Alaska*. Danbury, Conn.: Children's Press, 2002.

Strudwick, Leslie. *A Guide to Washington*. Mankato, Minn.: Weigl Publishers, Inc., 2001.

Places to visit

Crater Lake National Park (Oregon)
This lake was created by the eruption and collapse of Mount Mazama almost 7,000 years ago.

Death Valley National Park (California)
One of the hottest, driest, and lowest places on Earth.

Space Needle (Seattle, Washington)
Views from the top of this famous Seattle landmark include Puget Sound, the Olympic Mountains, and Mount Rainier.

Timeline

38,000 BC
The first nomadic hunters cross the land bridge from Asia to North America and set foot in Alaska.

10,000
Nomadic hunters enter Washington, Oregon, and California.

8000–2000
Inuits and Aleuts reach Alaska by boat from Asia.

AD 500
Polynesians from Marquesas Islands reach Hawaii.

1000
Polynesians from Tahiti reach Hawaii.

1542
Spanish navigator Juan Cabrillo reaches southern California.

1741
Vitus Bering and Russians reach the coast of Alaska.

1769
Father Junipero Serra establishes the first mission in California.

1778
Captain James Cook reaches Hawaii.

1805
Lewis and Clark reach Pacific Coast.

1812
Russians establish Fort Ross on the California coast.

1842
Pioneers begin migrating westward over the Oregon Trail.

1848
Gold is discovered at Sutter's Mill in California.

1867
William Seward purchases Alaska from Russia for $7.2 million.

1893
Queen Liliuokalani of Hawaii is deposed.

1897
Gold is discovered in the Klondike region of Yukon, near Alaska.

1900
Hawaii becomes a United States territory.

1906
San Francisco is hit by a great earthquake and fire.

1941
Japan attacks the United States naval base at Pearl Harbor in Hawaii.

1964
California becomes the most populous state in the country. A major earthquake hits Alaska.

1977
The Trans-Alaska pipeline across Alaska is completed at a cost of $7.7 billion to carry oil across the state.

1980
Mount St. Helens erupts. Ronald Reagan, former governor of California, is elected president.

1989
A major earthquake kills 60 people in the San Francisco Bay area.

1994
A major earthquake hits Los Angeles, killing 60 people.

States at a Glance

Alaska

Nickname: The Last Frontier, Land of the Midnight Sun
Became State: 1959
Capital: Juneau
Motto: North to the Future
Flower: Forget-me-not
Tree: Sitka spruce
Animal: Moose
Bird: Willow ptarmigan
Song: "Alaska's Flag"

California

Nickname: The Golden State
Became State: 1850
Capital: Sacramento
Motto: *Eureka* (I Have Found It)
Flower: Golden poppy
Tree: California redwood
Animal: Grizzly bear
Bird: California valley quail
Song: "I Love You, California"

Hawaii

Nickname: The Aloha State
Became State: 1959
Capital: Honolulu
Motto: *Ua Mau Ke Ea O Ka Aina I Ka Pono* (The life of the land is perpetuated in righteousness)
Flower: Yellow hibiscus
Tree: Kukui (Candlenut)
Animal: Humpback whale
Bird: Nene (Hawaiian goose)
Song: "Hawaii Ponoi"

Oregon

Nickname: Beaver State
Became State: 1859
Capital: Salem
Motto: She flies with her own wings
Flower: Oregon grape
Tree: Douglas fir
Animal: Beaver
Bird: Western meadowlark
Song: "Oregon, My Oregon"

Washington

Nickname: The Evergreen State
Became State: 1889
Capital: Olympia
Motto: *Al-ki* (Native American word meaning "bye and bye")
Flower: Coast (or Western) rhododendron
Tree: Western hemlock
Animal: Orca
Bird: Willow goldfinch (also known as wild canary)
Song: "Washington, My Home"

Glossary

Aleut member of the Native American group living in the Aleutian Islands in Alaska

arboretum place where trees, shrubs, and other plants are grown for scientific and educational purposes

breaching rising and breaking through the water surface

bristlecone pine oldest living tree on Earth

cable car vehicle on tracks, moved by a cable

climate weather conditions that are usual for a place

cuisine style of cooking

culture ideas, skills, arts, and a way of life of a certain people at a certain time

descent ancestry

diverse having variety

giant sequoia largest living tree on Earth

glacier large sheet of ice that spreads or retreats very slowly over land

Ice Age period of time when a large part of the earth was covered with huge sheets of ice (glaciers) and the temperatures were cooler

immigration act of moving to another country to settle

land bridge land connecting Alaska and Siberia during the last Ice Age when the sea level was much lower

migrant person who moves from place to place

mission church community set up by traveling priests called missionaries

monorail railway that runs on one rail

natural resources materials found in nature that are necessary or useful to people

nomadic hunter hunter who moved from place to place following herds of wild animals

northwest passage ice-free sea route that would allow passage of ships between the northern parts of the Atlantic and Pacific oceans

peninsula piece of land extending over a body of water

petroglyph ancient carving in rock

pictograph ancient painting on rock

populous having a large population

revenue money that a government receives from taxation

Richter scale scale for measuring an earthquake

salt flat type of desert flat land where the soil is too salty and dry for plants to grow

tectonic plates interlocking pieces of land that make up the continents on Earth

tradition custom or belief handed down from generation to generation

tsunami high sea wave caused by an earthquake or other major disturbance

Victorian style characteristic of the reign of Queen Victoria (1837–1901) of England

Index